How To Build High Performance IT Teams

Tips And Techniques That IT Managers Can Use In Order To Develop Productive Teams

"Practical, proven techniques that will help you to create highly productive IT teams"

Dr. Jim Anderson

Published by:
Blue Elephant Consulting
Tampa, Florida

Copyright © 2014 by Dr. Jim Anderson

All rights reserved. No part of this book may be reproduced of transmitted in any form or by any means, electronic or mechanical, including photocopying, recording or by any information storage and retrieval system without written permission of the publisher, except for inclusion of brief quotations in a review.

Printed in the United States of America

Library of Congress Control Number: 2016919757

ISBN-13: 978-1540611628

ISBN-10: 1540611620

Warning – Disclaimer

The purpose of this book is to educate and entertain. This book does not promise or guarantee that anyone following the ideas, tips, suggestions, techniques or strategies will be successful. The author, publisher and distributor(s) shall have neither liability nor responsibility to anyone with respect to any loss or damage caused, or alleged to be caused, directly or indirectly by the information contained in this book.

Recent Books By The Author

Product Management

- How Product Managers Can Sell More Of Their Product: Tips & Techniques For Product Managers To Better Understand How To Sell Their Product

- Product Development Lessons For Product Managers: How Product Managers Can Create Successful Products

Public Speaking

- Changing How You Speak To Overcome Your Fear Of Speaking: Change techniques that will transform a speech into a memorable event

- Delivering Excellence: How To Give Presentations That Make A Difference: Presentation techniques that will transform a speech into a memorable event

CIO Skills

- Keeping The Barbarians Out: How CIOs Can Secure Their Department and Company: Tips And Techniques For CIOs To Use In Order To Secure Both Their IT Department And Their Company

- What CIOs Need To Know In Order To Successfully Manage An IT Department: Decision Making Skills That Every CIO Needs To Have In Order To Be Able To Make The Right Choices

- How CIOs Can Make Innovation Happen: Tips And Techniques For CIOs To Use In Order To Make Innovation Happen In Their IT Department

IT Manager Skills

- Building The Perfect Team: What Staffing Skills Do IT Managers Need?: Tips And Techniques That IT Managers Can Use In Order To Correctly Staff Their Teams

- Secrets Of Effective Leadership For IT Managers: Tips And Techniques That IT Managers Can Use In Order To Develop Leadership Skills

Negotiating

- Use The Power Of Arguing To Win Your Next Negotiation: How To Develop The Skill Of Effective Arguing In A Negotiation In Order To Get The Best Possible Outcome

- Learn How To Signal In Your Next Negotiation: How To Develop The Skill Of Effective Signaling In A Negotiation In Order To Get The Best Possible Outcome

Miscellaneous

- How To Heal A Broken Leg – Fast!: Understanding how to deal with a broken leg in order to start walking again quickly

- How Software Defined Networking (SDN) Is Going To Change Your World Forever: The Revolution In Network Design And How It Affects

Note: See a complete list of books by Dr. Jim Anderson at the back of this book.

Acknowledgements

Any book like this one is the result of years of real-world work experience. In my over 25 years of working for 7 different firms, I have met countless fantastic people and I've been mentored by some truly exceptional ones. Although I've probably forgotten some of the people who made me the person that I am today, here is my attempt to finally give them the recognition that they so truly deserve:

- Thomas P. Anderson
- Art Puett
- Bobbi Marshall
- Bob Boggs

Dr. Jim Anderson

This book is dedicated to my family: Lori, Maddie, Nick, and Ben. None of this would have been possible without their constant love and support.

Thanks for always believing in me and providing me with the strength to always be willing to go out there and be my best for you.

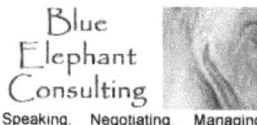
Speaking.   Negotiating.   Managing.   Marketing.

Table Of Contents

TEAMWORK IS YOUR KEY TO CAREER SUCCESS 9

ABOUT THE AUTHOR 11

CHAPTER 1: CLOUD WALKING: 5 WAYS TO MAKE THE CLOUD WORK FOR YOU 16

CHAPTER 2: IT MANAGERS KNOW WHEN TO USE A TEAM – AND WHEN NOT TO 20

CHAPTER 3: IT MANAGERS WANT TO KNOW WHAT MAKES A GOOD TEAM? 24

CHAPTER 4: IT MANAGERS NEED TO HAVE THE SKILLS TO MAKE TEAMWORK HAPPEN 28

CHAPTER 5: DOES YOUR TEAM KNOW THAT YOU APPRECIATE THEM? 32

CHAPTER 6: HOW SHOULD AN IT MANAGER SAY "THANKS"? 36

CHAPTER 7: WHY IT MANAGERS NEED TO BUILD TEAMS THAT ALL GENERATIONS WANT TO WORK ON 40

CHAPTER 8: WHY RITA IS WHAT IT MANAGERS SHOULD BE DOING TO BUILD BETTER TEAMS..44

CHAPTER 9: SECRETS TO BUILDING GREAT IT TEAMS 48

CHAPTER 10: WHY FAILING JUST MIGHT BE THE BEST THING TO EVER HAPPEN TO AN IT MANAGER 52

CHAPTER 11: THE 3 THINGS THAT YOUR TEAM REALLY WANTS FROM YOU 56

CHAPTER 12: HOW SHOULD IT MANAGERS TALK WITH MEMBERS OF THEIR TEAM? 60

Teamwork Is Your Key To Career Success

In order to be successful as an IT manager, you need to be able to show the company that under your leadership your team is able to deliver high quality products on time and under budget. If you want to have any chance of being able to pull this off, then you are going to have to discover ways to build a high performance IT team.

The arrival of cloud technology now makes keeping your team together and informed that much easier. IT managers need to understand that not all of the challenges that they face are going to require a team to solve. However, when a team is required, you are going to have to make sure that you have a good understanding of exactly what makes up a good team.

If you want to interact with your team correctly, then you are going to have to first make sure that you have the correct skills that this is going to require. Something that too many IT managers don't realize is that their teams are constantly looking for feedback that tells them that you appreciate them. This is not hard to do and in some cases can be as simple as remembering to tell them "thank you".

I'm not sure that there is just one secret to building a high performance IT team. However, the most important thing that you are going to have to do is to make sure that your team attracts members from all generations – you're going to need all of them to get the job done.

One of the most important skills that an IT manager needs to develop is the ability to talk with your team. By doing this correctly, you'll have a much better chance to discover just exactly what your team wants from you. This will also make it easier when you fail – and yes, you will fail because we all do. However, with the support of your team you'll be able to get right back up and keep moving forward.

For more information on what it takes to be a great IT manager, check out my blog, The Accidental IT Leader, at:

www.TheAccidentalITLeader.com

Good luck!

- Dr. Jim Anderson

About The Author

I must confess that I never set out to be a CIO. When I went to school, I studied Computer Science and thought that I'd get a nice job programming and that would be that. Well, at least part of that plan worked out!

My first job was working for Boeing on their F/A-18 fighter jet program. I spent my days programming fighter jet software in assembly language and I loved it. The U.S. government decided to save some money and went looking for other countries to sell this plane to. This put me into an unfamiliar role: I started to meet with foreign military officials and I ended up having to manage groups of engineers who were working on international projects.

Time moved on and so did I. I found myself working for Siemens, the big German telecommunications company. They were making phone switches and selling them to the seven U.S. phone companies. The problem was that the switches were too complicated. Customers couldn't tell the difference between one complicated phone switch from another complicated phone switch. Once again I found myself working with the sales and marketing teams to find ways to make the great technology that the engineers had developed understandable to both internal and external customers.

I've spent over 25 years working as an senior IT professional for both big companies and startups. This has given me an opportunity to learn what it takes to manage and IT department in ways that allow it to maximize its output while becoming a valuable part of the overall company.

I now live in Tampa Florida where I spend my time managing my consulting business, Blue Elephant Consulting, teaching college courses at the University of South Florida, and traveling to work with companies like yours to share the knowledge that I have about how to create and manage successful IT departments.

I'm always available to answer questions and I can be reached at:

Dr. Jim Anderson
Blue Elephant Consulting
Email: jim@BlueElephantConsulting.com
Facebook: http://goo.gl/1TVoK
Web: **www.BlueElephantConsulting.com**

"Unforgettable communication skills that will set your ideas free..."

Create IT Departments That Are Productive And A Valuable Asset To The Rest Of The Company!

Dr. Jim Anderson is available to provide training and coaching on the topics that are the most important to people who have to manage IT departments: how can I build a productive IT department (and keep it together) while at the same time providing the rest of the company with the IT services that they need?

Dr. Anderson believes that in order to both learn and remember what he says, speakers need to laugh. Each one of his speeches is full of fun and humor so that what he says "sticks" with everyone.

Dr. Anderson's CIO Skills Training Includes:

1. How to identify and attract the right type of IT workers to your IT department.
2. How to build relationships with the company's senior management in order to get the support that you need?
3. How to stay on top of changing technology and security issues so that you never get surprised?

Dr. Jim Anderson works with over 100 customers per year. To invite Dr. Anderson to work with you, contact him at:

Phone: 813-418-6970 or
Email: jim@BlueElephantConsulting.com

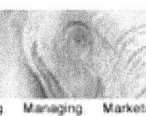

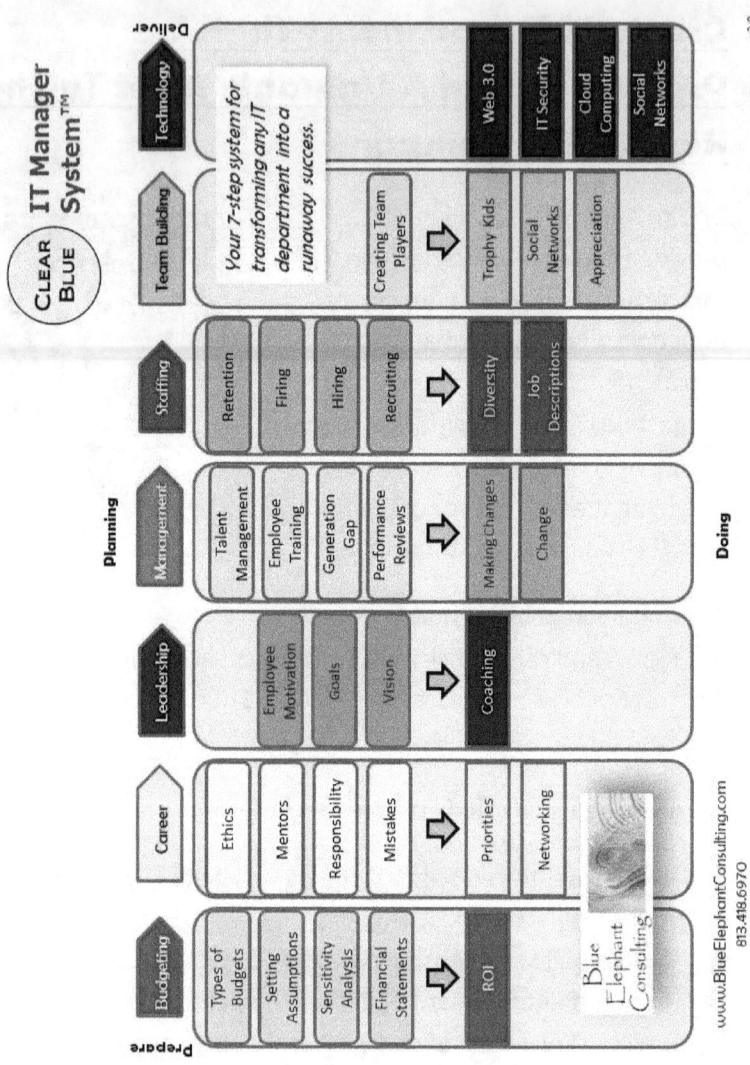

The **Clear Blue IT Manager System™** has been created to provide IT managers with a clear roadmap for how to manage an IT team. This system shows IT Managers what needs to be done and in what order to do it.

Chapter 1

Cloud Walking: 5 Ways To Make The Cloud Work For You

Chapter 1: Cloud Walking: 5 Ways To Make The Cloud Work For You

I'm guessing that the last thing in the world that you really need to be reading about right now is more "cloud" talk. The world of IT is experiencing a form of **"cloud fever"** in which every company seems to be talking about how they are going to use cloud computing to become more successful. Well, talk is cheap and in the end it's starting to look like nobody really has a clue as to how to go about actually doing this. How about if we lay down some practical steps that you can take to use the cloud to make your IT team more successful?

Step 1: Appoint A Cloud Champion

You're going to need to have someone step up and become a clear **cloud booster** in your organization. There's no problem with this being you – if you've got enough pull. If you don't then you need someone farther up the food chain to come forward and tell everyone that this is what we're going to do.

Step 2: Make Using The Cloud To Collaborate Mandatory

Come on, you know how us IT folks are – once we get used to doing something one way, we hate to change. Add on top of that collaboration tools who's primary purpose is to get us to share our hard learned information, well you can guess just how popular that idea is going to be.

You are going to have to change how your team gets compensated – using your cloud-based tools has got to **become a required part of everyone's job**. New polices like "you have to make three updates to our wiki each week" are the way to start things rolling.

Step 3: Focus And Share

Saying that you're going to start using cloud based tools to collaborate better without having a driving goal is the wrong way to go about doing this. Instead, **pick one set of information** that your IT team needs to do a better job of sharing and start by focusing on how that information is created. This is going to make it much easier for you to measure your success.

Step 4: In With The New, In With The Old

Just because your team starts to use some nice new shiny cloud based collaboration tools doesn't mean that you get to throw all of your old tools away. I'm going to bet that like most of the corporate world your team uses **Outlook** for email and it's going to be important that at the bare minimum that you find a way for your new tools to work with Outlook.

Step 5: Training, Training, Training

The best collaboration tool in the world isn't worth the code that it's written in **if nobody can figure out how to use it**. Unless you're using an app that was written by the user interface engineers at Apple, you're going to have to take the time (and expense) to make sure that everyone who is going to be using it knows how to get the most out of it.

What All Of This Means For You

Managing a team of individual IT workers who operate in **unconnected silos** is just about the hardest way to get anything done. As an IT Leader your task is to find ways to get everyone to share information and to work together.

Cloud based collaboration tools provide an excellent way for you to get your team to work together and **share information**. These tools are even more valuable if your team is distributed across multiple locations.

There are no **"silver bullets"** in IT. Cloud based collaboration tools are very useful, but unless your name is Harry Potter they aren't going to magically fix all of your team's issues. However, they are a step in the right direction and they may be the most important step for you to take…

Chapter 2

IT Managers Know When To Use A Team – And When Not To

Chapter 2: IT Managers Know When To Use A Team – And When Not To

If ever there was a trendy word in the world of IT management, it would have to be **the word "team"**. If you read enough books or listen to enough gurus, you'd have to be forgiven for coming away with the impression that the solution to just about every IT problem is to throw a team at it. Sure teams can be useful, but IT managers need to know when they work – and when they don't.

When Is A Team The Right Idea For An IT Manager?

Despite what you may have read, teams are not always the correct solution for every IT problem. In fact, you might not be **the right kind of IT manager** to be on a team.

How come teams don't always work? A lot of this has to do with **the way that a team is built**. If an IT manager doesn't (or isn't allowed to) correctly fund, staff, and run a team, then there is very little chance that it's going to be able to successfully accomplish its objective.

IT managers need to be careful about allowing themselves to **become part of a team**. How a team operates is much different from how an IT department operates. Whereas an IT manager is clearly in charge when it comes to determining what his staff does, the same cannot be said about a team. In fact, an IT manager might not even be in charge of the team.

The level of collaboration that it takes to make a team work is **significantly different** from how day-to-day IT management is performed. IT managers need to be aware of these types of differences.

When Is A Team The Right Idea For The People On It?

Maybe before we spend any time trying to determine when a team is the right way to go about solving a problem, we should first agree on just exactly **what a team is**. This should be easy, right?

It turns out that everyone **THINKS** that they know what a team is, but we all seem to have slightly different definitions. Let's agree that for our purposes a team is more than just a bunch of people who work together. Instead, let's define a team as being a collection of people who bring complementary skills together to work towards achieving a common goal.

So there we go, we've got a good feel for what a team is. Now all we need to do is to make sure that we understand when using a team is **the right decision** for solving an IT problem. It turns out that there are four main categories of challenges that are well suited for being solved by teams:

Different Skills Needed: problems that can only be solved by having a collection of IT workers who have a specific set of talents and skills that no one person has.

Hand-Offs: problems that require IT workers to work together with a great deal of back-and-forth exchanges in order to solve the problem.

Defined Deliverable: the problem must have a very clear deliverable that needs to be produced or delivered.

End Date: teams shouldn't last forever. The problem must have a "due by" date that lets everyone know exactly when the team's task will be completed.

What Does All Of This Mean For You?

The idea of using teams to solve every IT problem that an IT manager faces can be **dangerously seductive**. It's true that a lot of problems can be solved by teams, but we've got to realize that not every problem calls for a team.

IT managers need to take the time to first determine if creating a team that they are on **is a good idea**. How they manage and how they motivate the other members of the team may be very different from how they work as an IT manager. To correctly determine when a team should be used, IT managers need to be very aware of the four different types of problems that are best solved by teams.

As with any management tool, teams can be **a powerful way to solve problems**. However, IT managers need to first take the time to evaluate a problem and determine if it calls for a team based solution. Pick the right types of problems to apply a team to and you'll always come out a winner!

Chapter 3

IT Managers Want To Know What Makes A Good Team?

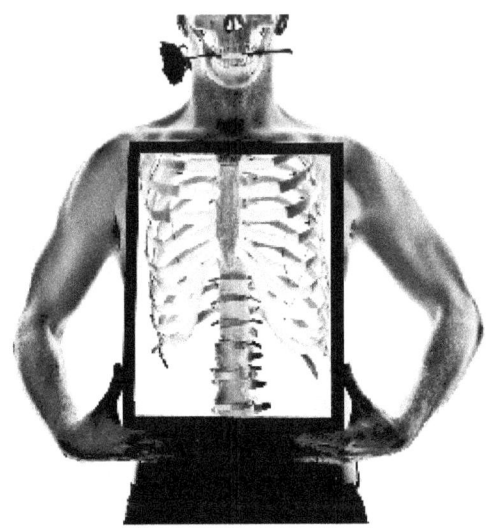

Chapter 3: IT Managers Want To Know What Makes A Good Team?

In order to maximize what you will be able to accomplish as an IT manager, you are going to have to be able to build effective teams. All too often when we are faced with a new challenge, we'll simply look around for who's available and **draft them to be on the team that we're putting together.** Is it any wonder that all too often our teams never accomplish what they set out to do?

What Are The Characteristics Of A Good Team?

If we can all agree that building a great team is a critical step in solving challenging IT problems, the next question that needs to be answered is **just what makes a great IT team great?** Sure, we all know that having the right people with the right set of skills is part of it, but is that all that we need?

It turns out that although that's an important part of the solution, it's really only one part and in fact it may not even be the most important part. What makes an IT team effective is a question on which a great deal of study has been done over the last few years. The good news is that all of the studies have reached basically the same conclusion: there are **6 key characteristics** of a team that will ensure that it is successful.

These 6 characteristics are as follows:

Technical Skills: every member of the team needs to bring a skill or a set of skills that will be vital to solving the problem at hand. No deadwood is permitted.

A Big Goal: there needs to be one overarching goal that everyone knows that they are working towards.

Commitment: each member of the team needs to have fully bought into what the team is trying to accomplish.

Mutual Gain: everyone on the team needs to realize that the only way that they are going to benefit from participating in the team is by contributing to accomplishing the team's goals.

Senior Support: it takes the support of the company and especially the company's senior management in order for a team to have a hope of being successful.

Coordination: the ability to align the team's efforts with what the rest of the company is trying to accomplish is critical so that outside resources can be leveraged in order to move the team closer to completing its goal.

The Importance Of Goals

Each of these characteristics of a successful IT team is important; however, **the one key** to building a successful team that cannot be overlooked is ensuring that there is a single goal for the team to pursue and that everyone knows what it is.

If you don't take the time to establish **a single clear goal for your team**, then the various members of your team will make up their own. This is a very natural thing for IT department employees to do. The problem with this is that they will probably all make up different goals for themselves. As they work towards these goals what will happen will be that they end up working at cross-purposes and the team is unable to move forward.

Additionally, even if a single goal is created and advertised to the team, it may not be enough. Each member of the team needs to **commit themselves to the goal**. By doing this and by "having some skin in the game", they will tie their reputation and their careers to the success of the team. This ensures that they will be motivated to work towards achieving the team's single goal.

What This All Means For You

IT managers need to have a wide variety of skills in order to be successful. Not only do they need to know how to lead an IT team, but they also need to know **how to build a successful team in the first place**.

It turns out that this is a problem that has been studied for a number of years. There are **six key characteristics** that every effective IT team needs to have. Chief among these characteristics is the need for a team to have a single goal that everyone can focus on. IT managers need to ensure that each member of the team has a commitment to achieving this goal.

It is possible to build an effective team. However, as an IT manager it requires you to **take the time** to carefully make sure that each member of the team that you select to be on the team meets the 6 criteria. If you do this, then you'll find yourself managing nothing but successful teams...!

Chapter 4

IT Managers Need To Have The Skills To Make Teamwork Happen

Chapter 4: IT Managers Need To Have The Skills To Make Teamwork Happen

Hopefully by now in your IT manager career you have reached the understanding that in order for your IT team to be successful, **they are all going to have to learn how to work together**. You know, that teamwork stuff. More often than not your team is not automatically going to know how to do this and that's when your teamwork IT manager skills are going to have to come into play...

6 Teamwork Skills That Every IT Manager Must Have

Isn't teamwork just something that sorta naturally happens? The answer is – sometimes. Yes, an IT team can just fall into place and everyone can seamlessly work together. However, all too often it doesn't happen that way. This is when you as an IT manager need to step in and **use your IT manager training to provide teamwork skills that will boost your team's productivity**. Here are the 6 skills that you're going to need in order to pull this off:

Leading a team: Yes, that's right – your IT team is not going to be going anywhere if they don't have a leader. Please note that just because you have the job title "IT manager" does not automatically make you a leader. You are going to have to earn the respect of your team and then you're going to have to always be showing them what they need to be doing. Note that if you do this well, then you'll take care of that IT team building thing at the same time.

Group problem solving: If one brain is good, then many brains are even better. No matter if the team is trying to solve a hard technical problem or they are just trying to sort out who within the team should be doing what, your ability to lead them through the problem solving process is what is going to allow them to solve the problem and move on.

Keeping teams on target: Welcome to the 21st Century in which every member of your IT team is online, plugged in, and constantly being distracted by a million different things. As the IT manager, you are going to have to teach your teams how they can keep their focus on what's really important.

Working with a virtual team: Did I mention that we are all working in the 21st Century these days? More and more often your IT team is not all going to be located in the same place. What this means is that you are going to have to be able to teach your team how to work together using email, conference bridges, Skype, etc. It can be done, it's just that you're going to have to show everyone how best to do it.

Assuming team membership roles: Unlike what you may have heard from others, not all members of an IT team are created equal. On a team everyone will play a different, but important, role. You are going to need your leaders, your followers, your note takers, your problem solvers, your researchers, etc. Making sure that everyone knows what role they are playing. Teaching everyone how that role supports everyone else on the team is your job to do.

Collaborating: On a team, no one person is going to be solving any given problem. Instead, you're going to have two or more of your team members working together, collaborating, to solve problems. What this means is that they are going to have to be taught by you how to communicate with each other and how to deal with interpersonal issues when they come up – like they always do!

What All Of This Means For You

The secret to a successful IT team is getting everyone to help each other to accomplish more than they would be able to accomplish by themselves. In other words, **get everyone to show some teamwork**.

What too many IT managers don't realize is that **many teams don't know how to make this happen**. That's why we need to develop our teamwork skills so that we can lead our team and teach them about group problem solving, collaborating, working virtually, and help them to understand the role that they'll play within the team.

You probably already have some of the teamwork skills that you need. Take a close look at our list and determine **which ones you still need to work on**. Remember that the better your teamwork skills are, the better your team will perform and ultimately the better that you'll look to the rest of your company.

Chapter 5

Does Your Team Know That You Appreciate Them?

Chapter 5: Does Your Team Know That You Appreciate Them?

Appreciation is a word that I believe that we're all familiar with, but do we really know what it means? More importantly, as IT managers do we **take the time to show the members of our team that we appreciate them and the work that they do**? If we're not doing this, then we're missing out on a great opportunity...

Why Appreciation Is So Important

As an IT manager, one of your most important IT manager skills is to **communicate clearly with your team**. I think that we all understand that we need to quickly step in and correct actions that team members are doing that are not right. However, I think that all too often we forget that there is another side to this – we also need to show appreciation for our team members when they do something right.

The beauty of showing appreciation is that **it really doesn't cost anything**. It also doesn't take a lot of time to do correctly. However, when you take the time to show appreciation for a member of your team, it can have a very large impact on them – they feel that their work is being noticed and their efforts are valued.

How you go about **showing appreciation** is up to you. There are countless ways to make this happen. Of course a face-to-face meeting is the most direct way. However, in today's distributed work environment you can also show your appreciation via a telephone call, an email, or even via a text message.

The Problem With Not Showing Appreciation

All too often we IT managers don't even think about showing appreciation to our team members. The reasons for this can be quite complex. More often than not, it comes down to the simple fact that during our career, **our bosses never showed us much appreciation** so we don't think to show it to our team members. We never got any IT manager training in how to show appreciation.

Another reason that some IT managers are hesitant to show appreciation is because they think that **they don't have to**. Their thinking goes that the members of their team are being paid to perform their jobs, why should any additional appreciation be required? The mistake here is that by showing some appreciation, there is a good chance that your team will do an even better job of performing their jobs.

At the end of the day, your job as an IT manager is to **inspire your team** to do their best work. The simple act of showing some appreciation can go a long way in making this happen. There is no good reason that showing appreciation should not be a part of your everyday manager activities.

What All Of This Means For You

As an IT manager it is your responsibility to keep your team motivated and performing **at their peak level**. Sure IT team building can help with this; however, limited budgets and the time crunch that most teams live under mean that we need to always be on the lookout for ways that we can tell our team that they are doing a good job. It turns out that appreciation is a great way to go about doing this.

Appreciation **doesn't cost anything** and it really does mean a lot to the members of your team. Many managers are hesitant to provide their team members with appreciation because they think that they don't need it. It turns out that appreciation is one of the most sought after things that all IT team members want.

In this life it is all too rare for a tool to come along that doesn't cost us anything to use. Appreciation is one such tool. Realize that the members of your team are **desperate for appreciation from you** and make sure that you give it to them. It's easy to do and you sure can't beat the price!

Chapter 6

How Should An IT Manager Say "Thanks"?

Chapter 6: How Should An IT Manager Say "Thanks"?

In the movie Dune the good guys come up with a sonic weapon called a Weirding Module that allows them to **transform their spoken word into a powerful weapon**. It turns out that among the IT manager skills that we have, we have powerful words at our command that if we know about them we can use to create powerful results.

The Power Of "Thanks"

If you were to take a poll of the members of your team and ask them what attributes of their job they felt were **the most important**, what answers do you think that you'd get? A lot of us would assume that salary would be #1 on any list that we got. However, we'd be wrong.

When such surveys are conducted, the #1 desired job feature, by a wide margin, has always been the need to feel appreciated. Since this is such a big deal to our team members, **it needs to be a big deal for IT managers**. We had better get good at showing some appreciation to the people who work on our teams. Too bad none of us have ever had any IT manager training on how best to go about doing this.

It turns out that this is not all that hard to do. Simply saying "thanks" when someone on your team does a good job can be what they are looking for. As simple as this action sounds, **the results can be amazing**. Likewise, if you are a manager who never takes the time to thank your team members you may discover that people start to leave your team.

How To Use The Power Of Thanks

It turns out that using the power of "thanks" is just a little bit more complicated than just remembering to say the word every so often. In order to do this right, the person that you are talking with **is going to have to truly believe that you mean it**. There are two steps to the process and you're going to have to do them both.

First, **you are going to have to be very clear about what you are thanking the person for**. Just exactly what behavior, performance, or action did they do that you feel deserves a thanks. Next, you're going to have to tell them why their action deserves your appreciation and the positive business impact that it's going to have.

I fully realize that this may look like I'm taking something that should be simple and I'm making it seem harder than it should be. However, the power of thanks comes from the fact that the person that you're telling it to **really believes that you mean it**. Follow these steps and you'll have yet one more powerful manager tool to use.

What All Of This Means For You

As IT managers we may often feel that **our hands are tied** in terms of how we can reward our teams. Funds for IT team building activities are limited, raises are on hold, and our competitors seem to be offering a better work environment. What's a manager to do?

It turns out that what our team members really want is for us to **acknowledge their accomplishments**. We can do this by simply remembering to tell them "thanks" when they've done a good job. Appreciating them for what they've done will go a very long way in boosting their job satisfaction.

Being a successful IT manager **comes down to doing the little things correctly**. Showing appreciation to your team by telling them "thanks" when they deserve it is part of this. Look for opportunities to acknowledge accomplishments and you'll start to develop a reputation as an IT manager who "gets it".

Chapter 7

Why IT Managers Need To Build Teams That All Generations Want To Work On

Chapter 7: Why IT Managers Need To Build Teams That All Generations Want To Work On

IT managers dread the day that they have to manage certain generations – we don't have the IT manager skills to deal with this situation. Whatever generation the IT manager belongs to should be easy to manage – they know how that generation thinks. **It's all the other generations that cause the problems**. However, it turns out that what we need to be doing is building teams that are open to all generations. Just exactly how are we supposed to go about doing that?

How We Like To Communicate

As an IT manager one of the most important things that you need to realize about managing multiple generations is that **we all communicate differently**. In the modern workplace there are multiple different ways that we can share information with each other and we all have different preferences as to how we accomplish this.

The younger generations, the millennials, like to use **the most modern of communication tools**. These are the employees who will tweet their questions and use Instagram and Snapchat to connect with other members of their teams. The slightly older Generation X members of your team will prefer to use email for almost all of their communications. Finally, the baby boomers will rely on voice conversations conducted over the telephone or in person.

As an IT manager you need to appreciate that **everyone will have their own preferred means of being contacted**. Instead of trying to get everyone to conform to one method, your job is to facilitate the communication between team members. One way to make this happen is to create and distribute a spreadsheet that lists each person on your team and their preferred method of being contacted. It turns out that most people will get in touch with each other using the preferred method if they know that the person has a preference.

How We Like To Be Managed

All of that IT manager training that we've had dealt with IT team building but never really taught us how to deal with trying to manage people **who had very definite ideas about how they wanted to be managed**. When you are managing a team that has multiple generations on it, you're going to have a challenge because each generation has their own ideas about how they want to be managed.

You are going to be **dealing with two differing approaches** to how your team wants to be managed. The older members of your team are going to believe that everyone needs to earn their place on the team and that this takes time – you have to work your way up the ladder. The younger members of your team are going to want to have their voices heard right off the bat – they don't want to have to wait to reach a certain level for their thoughts to be part of the decision making process.

One way to handle this challenge is to **create a flat management structure** to use for your team. This can allow leaders to emerge on a per project basis depending on each worker's unique set of skills and talents.

What All Of This Means For You

IT managers are facing a challenge that has not been seen in the workplace before: we have **three different generations** that are all working together. It is our responsibility to build teams that are inviting to each generation and allows them to work together.

A key part of making this happen is to understand that **everyone likes to communicate differently**. Acknowledge this and make it easy for everyone to know how everyone wants to be reached. Projects need to have a flexible management structure. The younger workers will want a way for their voices to be heard and you need to accommodate that.

The good news is that as an IT manager **you've got an incredibly diverse workforce to choose from**. Your big challenge will be in creating teams that people want to join. Take the time to understand the needs of each generation and you'll be the IT manager that everyone wants to work for...

Chapter 8

Why RITA Is What IT Managers Should Be Doing To Build Better Teams

Chapter 8: Why RITA Is What IT Managers Should Be Doing To Build Better Teams

As an IT manager you have always be looking for people that you would like to add to your team. However, once you've used you IT manager skills to find them, convinced them to join your team, and actually gotten then on board, what should your next step be? It turns out that the answer is RITA...

What Is RITA?

All too often IT managers think that all that they have to do in order to add great talent to their team is to find the right person and invite them to join. There is very little IT manager training that teaches us how to do this correctly. Sorry about this, there's more to building a great team than just finding the right people. There are four distinct steps to effectively adding someone to your team. The acronym RITA is a great reminder of just exactly what you need to do: Recruit, Induct, Train, and Assess.

With a little luck you and your company are already doing a good job of recruiting new people to join your team. If you find yourself agonizing over trying to decide between two equally highly qualified candidates, then your recruitment program is doing a good job. The next step is to induct the people that you select. Induction is how you share your team's culture with new recruits. Culture is what drives people's actions when you're not watching them.

The next step is to train your new recruits. The ultimate goal of your training needs to be to let the new members of your team know how you want them to behave. If you don't tell them, then they'll never know.

How Do You Get People To Really Join Your Team?

When someone agrees to become part of your team, that's a good start. However, as an IT manager what you want them to do is to fully commit to joining the team. What's it going to take to make this happen?

An important part of any new team member training program is to assign them a mentor. Having a mentor gives them someone that they can come to and talk confidentially with about any challenges that they are running into as they work to join the team. Additionally, any new member training program has to include some IT team building activities so that new and old team members can mix and meet.

I've always agreed with the saying that "Culture eats strategy for breakfast." As an IT manager you need to understand that when it comes to your new recruits it is going to be much easier for you to make corrections and keep the team's culture on track than to try to replace a wrong culture. After someone has been a member of your team for three months take a step back and ask yourself if they are truly on board or do you have more work to do here?

What Does All Of This Mean For You?

IT managers need to understand that just attracting people to join their team is not enough. They need to go the extra distance and actually make the new people part of their team after they have joined. This is not easy to do.

The experts recommend that we implement the RITA method: recruit, induct, train, and assess. In order to make new members of your team feel as though they belong, you are going to have tell them what you want them to be doing and provide them with mentors.

If you are thinking that all of this onboarding sounds like a lot of effort, you are correct. However, taking the time to make it happen now will yield fantastic results later on. Use the RITA method to build a great team!

Chapter 9

Secrets To Building Great IT Teams

Chapter 9: Secrets To Building Great IT Teams

As an IT manager, you can only be as good as your team allows you to be. This means that you are going to have use your IT manager skills and invest your time in making your team as good as you possibly can. Even if you can commit to doing this, the next question is **just exactly what should you be doing to make this happen?**

Building A Better Team

Your team is not going to be in a position to support you if you don't have the right team in place. This all has to do with **team dynamics** – how well do the members of your team work together? What you are looking for is a team that can be very cohesive. However, this is not just going to magically happen.

Instead, **it's all about who you hire to join your team**. It can be all too easy during the hiring process to go looking for the most competent person. However, that can turn out to be a mistake. All too often the most competent person may end up not getting along with the rest of your team. That's not going to be good for anyone and there is no IT manager training on how to avoid doing this.

In order to find the right person to join your team you need to know how to go about hiring them correctly. The best way is to be willing to **invest the time** that this is going to take.

I recommend that you **plan on spending at least an hour with every candidate that you are considering**. The reason for this is that by talking with them for an hour, the most amazing things can come to the surface. Anyone can fake it, but most of us can't fake it for an hour – our true personality will come to the surface eventually.

The Secret To Creating A Mission-Based Team

In order to create a team that is really going to be able to accomplish everything that you throw at them and support you in your goals, **you need to create a mission based team**. Having a mission for your team allows the individual members of your team to rally around the mission and it can pull all of them together.

What this means for you is that each member of your team is going to have to have **a strong moral compass**. They are going to have to be true believers in whatever mission you have selected for your team. To pull this off is going to take more than just talent.

As the IT manager, you have a critical role to play. You have to be **restating what the endgame for the team is**. By reminding the team what they are trying to achieve, you'll be able to get them to more fully commit to their jobs.

The final thing for you to realize just might the most difficult to put into practice. You need to clearly communicate to your team that **the mission of the team matters more than the money**. Yes, yes – the company is going to be sending them a different message, but you need to be very clear about this. If you want them to truly believe in what you want the team to accomplish, they need to understand that for you, it's all about the mission.

What All Of This Means For You

This IT team building stuff is hard to do! As an IT manager, you are responsible for creating a team that is going to be able to accomplish everything that you ask them to do and make you look good. This means that **you're going to have to have a special set of skills**.

Team dynamics are a very important part of any well performing team. Creating a team like this **starts with the hiring process**. Take the time to really talk to your job candidates in order to get to know them. Creating a mission-based team will provide your team with a reason to come to work every day. Make sure that you get the culture right, constantly restate the endgame, and make sure that you put the mission before the money.

If you are willing to take the time to build **a powerful and effective team**, then your IT manager career will go far. There won't be anything that can be thrown at your team that they won't be able to handle. Won't that make you look good?

Chapter 10

Why Failing Just Might Be The Best Thing To Ever Happen To An IT Manager

Chapter 10: Why Failing Just Might Be The Best Thing To Ever Happen To An IT Manager

Failure is bad, right? I mean, as IT leaders, we try to spend every day using our IT manager skills to find ways to allow our team to accomplish more – to be successful, **not a failure**. However, the harsh reality of life is that yes, sometimes we do fail. Does this mean that it's "game over" for us? Interestingly enough, no – in fact failing might be just exactly what we need do in order to become a success.

Just Exactly What Is A Failure?

Perhaps we should start our discussion by taking a look at **just exactly what a failure is**. I think that in our minds, we view failure as being a bad thing that our teams need to avoid at all costs. However, it can be just a bit too easy to forget just exactly what failure looks like as we start to try to avoid anything that we think might look just a little bit like failure.

I define failure as being when either we as a IT manager or our IT teams (or perhaps both of us together) **are not able to achieve something that we were trying to accomplish**. It really is as simple as that. If you can accept my definition of failure, then you just might start to realize that all of us fail a lot more often than we might normally think that we do.

However, if we are failing all of the time, then that means that all of the other IT teams at our company are probably also spending a considerable amount of their time failing also. This poses a bit of a dilemma, if we are all wallowing in failure as much as our definition would lead us to believe, then **how can** we ever possibility hope to have our IT teams become a success?

How Can You Make Failure A Good Thing?

If we can't stop our IT teams from failing, then we probably should look into seeing if it might be possible to find a way to **transform our failures into something more positive**. The good news is that this actually is possible. We just need a few suggestions on how best to go about doing this.

The first thing that you need to realize as an IT manager is that your IT team knows when it has failed. They fully understand when they were trying to achieve something and the team fell short. Nobody feels good when this happens and if you don't do something, then it's going to cause problems. You need to create a forum for your team where they can come and **confess when they have failed**. This has to be a nurturing, supportive environment where everyone can come together and where everyone feels comfortable standing up and telling everyone what they did that didn't work out so well.

The ability to come to grips with our failures is a critical first step for your team. The ability to share a failure with your peers allows you to **get it off of your shoulders**. When you hear about their failures you start to understand that you are not alone in not always being able to achieve everything that you wanted to do. This is a critical part of understanding what went wrong. By sharing your failure you'll be able to get the support of the rest of the team and they'll know to step in the next time you are struggling with a similar problem. They'll want you to succeed and this means that your chances of being successful next time are a lot higher.

What Does All Of This Mean For You?

As an IT manager, your job is to find ways to get your team to help the company move forward and become more profitable. As hard as you try, not all of your team's activities will always result in success. **In fact, sometimes you'll probably fail.** However, what you need to realize is that this is a part of life – failure is what opens the door to future successes.

We need to understand just exactly what a failure is. It is simply not being able to achieve something that we were trying to accomplish. The fact that we failed does not mean that we can't do it; rather, **it means that the way that we tried to do it was the wrong way.** In the spirit of IT team building what you need to do as an IT manager is to set up an environment where your team members will feel comfortable confessing to their failures. By doing this they'll be getting rid of negative feelings and sharing their experiences with the rest of the team.

Failures happen. You need to use your IT manager training to find ways to **turn these events into something that is going to help your team to improve.** Giving your team the confidence to admit to their failures and to share them with the rest of the team is a great way to help the team to move forward. Give this a try and see if you can change the team's failures into a very special kind of success.

Chapter 11

The 3 Things That Your Team Really Wants From You

Chapter 11: The 3 Things That Your Team Really Wants From You

So what is your job as an IT manager? What is it that your company is really paying you to do? There may be many different answers to this question, but at the end of the day **it's your job to use your IT manager skills to convince a group of IT professions to all work on what you tell them they need to do and to do a good job.** Although on the surface this may seem easy, as we all know it's fairly difficult to do well. However, it turns out that all your IT team wants from you is three things...

A Sense Of Purpose

As a company or even as an IT manager it can be all too easy to think that what the members of your IT team really want is more money. Don't get me wrong here, yes – everyone would like more money. But, if we're talking about what is going to give the members of your team a long term sense of motivation, then what you are going to have to provide them with is a sense of purpose. What this means for you as an IT manager is that the people on your team don't just want a job. **They want to work for a company that knows what it is trying to accomplish** and where what is right and what is wrong is well understood.

Some Autonomy

Now this is where things can get just a little bit tricky. As the leader of an IT team, you basically know how you want things done – that's what your IT manager training has taught you. Because of that, it can be all too easy to create your own solutions to the challenges that your team is facing. Once you do this, you no longer really need your team's inputs on how best to solve a problem. This can be a fundamental problem. The reason is because in any technical job, **the freedom for the members of your team to make their own decisions about how to solve a problem** is what is going to make them fall in love with their job over and over again.

Empathy, Please

Your team members are never going to love the company that they work for. How can they? The company does not have the ability to love them back. Instead, with a little luck they will love having you as their manager and they will love working on your team. In order to make this happen, you are going to have to take the time to **create a work environment that everyone is going to want to be a part of**. Can anyone say IT team building? This means that you need to welcome them in a big way on the day that they join your team, you are going to have remember and celebrate every anniversary, and when it comes to team members asking for time off, you are going to have to be flexible.

What All Of This Means For You

Managing a team of IT professionals is hard work. These are sophisticated people who all have different needs and wants. Because of their skill sets, they can pretty much leave and go get a different job tomorrow. What this means for you as an IT manager is that you are going to need to **find out what they are looking for from you in order to get them to stay and do productive work**.

The good news for you is that **there are just three things that every IT team member is looking to get out of their current job**. This starts with working for a company that can provide them with a true sense of purpose. Next they'd like some autonomy to create and implement their own solutions to problems. Finally, if you as their IT manager could show them some empathy then they would be able to return the feeling.

As an IT manager you have a great deal on your plate. Your management has expectations of what your IT team is going to be able to produce and you need to deliver. However, at the same time **you are going to have to work to make sure that each member of your team feels that this is the right job for them**. Follow these three tips and you'll have a happy and productive IT team.

Chapter 12

How Should IT Managers Talk With Members Of Their Team?

Chapter 12: How Should IT Managers Talk With Members Of Their Team?

The secret to being a good IT manager is having the IT manager skills to **truly connect with the members of your team**. This is not magic, it's actually a skill that can be learned with a little bit of IT manager training. You need to be able to sit down with each member of your team and have a real, meaningful conversation with them. This is the only way that you're going to be able to get them to believe in you and do what you need them to do for you. So just exactly how does one go about having these types of conversations?

You Gotta Prepare

All too often we lump talking with members of our team with all of the other things that we have on our plate to do. The reality is that this task is actually a great deal more important. Because of its importance we need to **take the time to prepare for each one of our team member discussions**. What you are going to want to do is to map out how you want the conversation to go. What are the issues that need to be discussed? What objections could be brought up and how should you respond to them. Finally, what are your goals for having this conversation in the first place?

You Really Don't Know It All

Once upon a time you were the member of an IT team. What this means is that there is a real possibility that you might think that you know everything that the team member that you'll be talking to is going to say. I mean, you've had their job and you've faced all of the challenges that they are currently facing – or so you think. The reality is that we are all different. You might think that you know what is going on in your team member's head, **but you really don't**. Learn to keep your mouth shut during the discussion that you have with them. Let them say what they want to tell you – don't make the mistake of believing that you already know what they are going to be saying or even why they'll be saying it.

Get Ready To Ask "Why"?

A lot of IT managers try to avoid conversations with team members because they don't know how they are going to keep the discussion going. I've got some good news for you: relax. It turns out that you already know how to keep these types of discussions going because you are not the one who should be doing the majority of the talking – you really want your team member to be doing that. In order to make this happen, **you need to get good at asking "why" in a 100 different ways**. This question can't be answered with a simple "yes / no" and will require your team member to think and then launch into a discussion with you. Job done!

What All Of This Means For You

The company expects you to accomplish a lot as an IT manager. The trick is that you really won't be doing much at all – **it's all about your team**. What this means is that you are going to have to be able to connect with each one of them (think of this as a form of IT team building) and find a way to motivate them to do what you need them to do for you. Looks like you are going to have to get good at the art of conversation…

There are **a number of different skills** that you are going to have to work at in order to be able to have good conversations with your team members. These include not just walking into a conversation – you will have to take the time to prepare for them. During the conversation you are going to have to keep reminding yourself that you really don't know it all and the person that you are talking with might have some valuable information for you. Finally, in order to dive deeper and deeper into the conversation you are going to have to become comfortable with asking "why" over and over again.

Surprisingly, many IT managers are not good at having conversations with their team members. This opens up a window for you to take the time to **master this art** and show the company that you can really connect with the members of your team. Once you get good at this, the way that your team performs will show how good of a manager you really are.

It's from the forge of failure that the steel of success is formed.

Hard Work Does Not Guarantee Success, But Success Does Not Happen Without Hard Work.

– Dr. Jim Anderson

Create IT Departments That Are Productive And A Valuable Asset To The Rest Of The Company !

Dr. Jim Anderson is available to provide training and coaching on the topics that are the most important to people who have to manage IT departments: how can I build a productive IT department (and keep it together) while at the same time providing the rest of the company with the IT services that they need?

Dr. Anderson believes that in order to both learn and remember what he says, speakers need to laugh. Each one of his speeches is full of fun and humor so that what he says "sticks" with everyone.

Dr. Anderson's CIO Skills Training Includes:

1. How to identify and attract the right type of IT workers to your IT department.
2. How to build relationships with the company's senior management in order to get the support that you need?
3. How to stay on top of changing technology and security issues so that you never get surprised?

Dr. Jim Anderson works with over 100 customers per year. To invite Dr. Anderson to work with you, contact him at:

Phone: 813-418-6970 or
Email: jim@BlueElephantConsulting.com

Photo Credits:

Cover - www.hacienda-la-colora.com
https://www.flickr.com/photos/xavier33300/15046006669/

Chapter 1 – theaucitron
https://www.flickr.com/photos/theaucitron/

Chapter 2 – Ethan
https://www.flickr.com/photos/ekavet/

Chapter 3 – Bernhard
https://www.flickr.com/photos/bernhard_jank/

Chapter 4 - Scott Maxwell
https://www.flickr.com/photos/lumaxart/

Chapter 5 - drinks machine
https://www.flickr.com/photos/drinksmachine/

Chapter 6 - Vern Hart
https://www.flickr.com/photos/vernhart/

Chapter 7 - David Lounsbury
https://www.flickr.com/photos/technodad/

Chapter 8 - Tim Ellis
https://www.flickr.com/photos/tim_ellis/

Chapter 9 – jacquelinetinney
https://www.flickr.com/photos/jacquelinetinney/

Chapter 10 - Behrooz Nobakht
https://www.flickr.com/photos/behruz/

Chapter 11 - Hubert Figuière
https://www.flickr.com/photos/hfiguiere/

Chapter 12 - {lor}
https://www.flickr.com/photos/lorigraphy/

Other Books By The Author

Product Management

- How Product Managers Can Sell More Of Their Product: Tips & Techniques For Product Managers To Better Understand How To Sell Their Product

- How To Create A Successful Product That Customers Will Want: Techniques For Product Managers To Boost Product Sales And Increase Customer Satisfaction

- What Product Managers Need To Know About World-Class Product Development: How Product Managers Can Create Successful Products

- How Product Managers Can Learn To Understand Their Customers: Techniques For Product Managers To Better Understand What Their Customers Really Want

- Product Management Secrets: Techniques For Product Managers To Boost Product Sales And Increase Customer Satisfaction

- Product Development Lessons For Product Managers: How Product Managers Can Create Successful Products

- Customer Lessons For Product Managers: Techniques For Product Managers To Better Understand What Their Customers Really Want

- Product Failure Lessons For Product Managers: Examples Of Products That Have Failed For Product Managers To Learn From

- Communication Skills For Product Managers: The Communication Skills That Product Managers Need To Know How To Use In Order To Have A Successful Product

- How To Have A Successful Product Manager Career: The Things That You Need To Be Doing TODAY In Order To Have A Successful Product Manager Career

- Product Manager Product Success: How to keep your product on track and make it become a success

Public Speaking

- Changing How You Speak To Overcome Your Fear Of Speaking: Change techniques that will transform a speech into a memorable event

- Delivering Excellence: How To Give Presentations That Make A Difference: Presentation techniques that will transform a speech into a memorable event

- Tools Speakers Need In Order To Give The Perfect Speech: What tools to use to create your next speech so that your message will be remembered forever!

- How To Create A Speech That Will Be Remembered

- Secrets To Organizing A Speech For Maximum Impact: How to put together a speech that will capture and hold your audience's attention

- How To Become A Better Speaker By Changing How You Speak: Change techniques that will transform a speech into a memorable event

- How To Give A Great Presentation: Presentation techniques that will transform a speech into a memorable event

- How To Rehearse In Order To Give The Perfect Speech: How to effectively rehearse your next speech to that your message be remembered forever!

- Secrets To Creating The Perfect Speech: How to create a speech that will make your message be remembered forever!

- Secrets To Organizing The Perfect Speech: How to organize the best speech of your life!

- Secrets To Planning The Perfect Speech: How to plan to give the best speech of your life

- How To Show What You Mean During A Presentation: How to use visual techniques to transform a speech into a memorable event

CIO Skills

- Keeping The Barbarians Out: How CIOs Can Secure Their Department and Company: Tips And Techniques For CIOs To Use In Order To Secure Both Their IT Department And Their Company

- What CIOs Need To Know In Order To Successfully Manage An IT Department: Decision Making Skills That Every CIO Needs To Have In Order To Be Able

To Make The Right Choices

- Becoming A Powerful And Effective Leader: Tips And Techniques That IT Managers Can Use In Order To Develop Leadership Skills

- CIO Secrets For Growing Innovation: Tips And Techniques For CIOs To Use In Order To Make Innovation Happen In Their IT Department

- Your Success As A CIO Depends On How Well You Communicate: Tips And Techniques For CIOs To Use In Order To Become Better Communicators

- What CIOs Need To Know About Working With Partners: Techniques For CIOs To Use In Order To Be Able To Successfully Work With Partners

- Critical CIO Management Skills: Decision Making Skills That Every CIO Needs To Have In Order To Be Able To Make The Right Choices

- How CIOs Can Make Innovation Happen: Tips And Techniques For CIOs To Use In Order To Make Innovation Happen In Their IT Department

- CIO Communication Skills Secrets: Tips And Techniques For CIOs To Use In Order To Become

Better Communicators

- Managing Your CIO Career: Steps That CIOs Have To Take In Order To Have A Long And Successful Career

- CIO Business Skills: How CIOs can work effectively with the rest of the company!

<u>IT Manager Skills</u>

- Save Yourself, Save Your Job – How To Manage Your IT Career: Secrets That IT Managers Can Use In Order To Have A Successful Career

- Growing Your CIO Career: How CIOs Can Work With The Entire Company In Order To Be Successful

- How IT Managers Can Make Innovation Happen: Tips And Techniques For IT Managers To Use In Order To Make Innovation Happen In Their Teams

- Staffing Skills IT Managers Must Have: Tips And Techniques That IT Managers Can Use In Order To Correctly Staff Their Teams

- Secrets Of Effective Leadership For IT Managers: Tips And Techniques That IT Managers Can Use In

Order To Develop Leadership Skills

- IT Manager Career Secrets: Tips And Techniques That IT Managers Can Use In Order To Have A Successful Career

- IT Manager Budgeting Skills: How IT Managers Can Request, Manage, Use, And Track Their Funding

- Secrets Of Managing Budgets: What IT Managers Need To Know In Order To Understand How Their Company Uses Money

Negotiating

- Use The Power Of Arguing To Win Your Next Negotiation: How To Develop The Skill Of Effective Arguing In A Negotiation In Order To Get The Best Possible Outcome

- Learn How To Signal In Your Next Negotiation: How To Develop The Skill Of Effective Signaling In A Negotiation In Order To Get The Best Possible Outcome

- Learn The Skill Of Exploring In A Negotiation: How To Develop The Skill Of Exploring What Is Possible In A Negotiation In Order To Reach The Best

Possible Deal

- Learn How To Argue In Your Next Negotiation: How To Develop The Skill Of Effective Arguing In A Negotiation In Order To Get The Best Possible Outcome|

- How To Open Your Next Negotiation: How To Start A Negotiation In Order To Get The Best Possible Outcome

- Preparing For Your Next Negotiation: What You Need To Do BEFORE A Negotiation Starts In Order To Get The Best Possible Deal

- Learn How To Package Trades In Your Next Negotiation

- All Good Things Come To An End: How To Close A Negotiation - How To Develop The Skill Of Closing In Order To Get The Best Possible Outcome From A Negotiation

- Take No Prisoners In Your Next Negotiation: How To Start A Negotiation In Order To Get The Best Possible Outcome

Miscellaneous

- How To Heal A Broken Leg – Fast!: Understanding how to deal with a broken leg in order to start walking again quickly

- How Software Defined Networking (SDN) Is Going To Change Your World Forever: The Revolution In Network Design And How It Affects You

- The Power Of Virtualization: How It Affects Memory, Servers, and Storage: The Revolution In Creating Virtual Devices And How It Affects You

- The Internet-Enabled Successful School District Superintendent: How To Use The Internet To Boost Parental Involvement In Your Schools

- Power Distribution Unit (PDU) Secrets: What Everyone Who Works In A Data Center Needs To Know!

- Making The Jump: How To Land Your Dream Job When You Get Out Of College!

- How To Use The Internet To Create Successful Students And Involved Parents

"Tips And Techniques That IT Managers Can Use In Order To Develop Productive Teams"

This book has been written with one goal in mind – to show you how an IT manager can build high performance teams. It's not easy being an IT manager so we're going to show you what you need to be doing in order create teams that can work together and deliver results!

Let's Make Your IT Career A Success!

What You'll Find Inside:

- DOES YOUR TEAM KNOW THAT YOU APPRECIATE THEM?

- WHY IT MANAGERS NEED TO BUILD TEAMS THAT ALL GENERATIONS WANT TO WORK ON

- WHY FAILING JUST MIGHT BE THE BEST THING TO EVER HAPPEN TO AN IT MANAGER

- THE 3 THINGS THAT YOUR TEAM REALLY WANTS FROM YOU

Dr. Jim Anderson brings his 25 years of real-world experience to this book. He's been an IT manager at some of the world's largest firms. He's going to show you what you need to do (and not do!) in order to successfully manage your career!

www.ingramcontent.com/pod-product-compliance
Lightning Source LLC
Chambersburg PA
CBHW061201180526
45170CB00002B/900